HEALTHY WAYS TO WORK FROM HOME

Derrick Chandler

CONTENTS

PREFACE

Working from the home heralds a new dawn in the way we work. This reality has never been more obvious than these trying time of a global pandemic. just like most things in our lives, the way we work would be seriously alterd post-pandemic. working from home seems to be the new deal. hoevre, like everything njovel, there would be several challenges and adjustments. This books zooms in on the health challenges that comes with working from home and suggestes various steps we can take to make our home office a more healthier place to work.

WORK FROM HOME: THE NEW REALITY?

The global job market is currently being inundated with fast-sweeping changes. As technology continues to re-shape our world, altering conventional ways of doing things, a plethora of challenges and opportunities would no doubt be brought to the fore. The threat of job automation continues to pose a threat considering the fact that about 60 percent of the global workforce may lose their jobs to the intrusion of technology.

At the same time, technology is also improving many labour markets. Telecommuting opportunities have expanded the ways employers and workers can connect, and are now available to organizations far beyond tech-industry. Tools like productivity software and virtual phone systems allow anyone with an internet connection have the same access as an office worker. This erstwhile unavailable ability to telecommute has allowed a variety of workers to follow career paths previously unavailable to them because of physical location, disability or even family structure.

Working from home seems to be the new reality of the global corporate machinery. While Work from Home – WFH - began to gain momentum and recognition during the coronavirus pandemic, no thanks to social distancing rules and technologies such as Skype, Zoom and Slack, it has in fact been in practice for decades with an increasing number of people choosing to adopt this new work pattern.

The preconceived notion of work as a place one goes to is rapidly being eroded as one does not need to be present at the work place full-time to execute tasks or be productive. In fact, many kinds of work can be executed effectively from the comfort of a home office. Tech giant, Twitter embracing the unprecedented changes brought about by technology and the global pandemic, has adopted a WFH policy, saying that its staff have the option to permanently work from home.

The social media company is just a point in the growing continuum of organizations that are embracing the new reality of work. More organizations seduced by a spike in employee productivity and reduced operating costs are embracing this new work culture. Other organizations such as Shopify, Facebook and Google are following suit.

Employees on their own part are happy they can spend more time with family, work within a flexible time frame, don't have to commute to work daily or deal with the ever-ticking bomb of office politics. WFH seems like a win-win situation for all stakeholders.

However, like any novel phenomenon, there are bound to be challenges let alone resistance from some quarters to this new work pattern. Some have argued against altering the traditional notion of work citing its implications for career development, job security and health – the latter of which this book deals with.

There are growing concerns that remote work has unforeseen implications for physical, social and mental health. Working in isolation, not getting enough physical activity and overcommitting oneself to various jobs are some of the factors which adversely affect the health of telecommuters.

This book looks at WFH as the new reality of work and analyses its implication on personal health. It looks at the benefits and de-merits of working from home, and includes strategies for work-ing in an efficient and productive manner from home without sacrificing one's health.

WHAT YOU DO, NOT WHERE YOU GO TO

For most people who grew up in the post-industrial revolution era where cottage industries were replaced by factory work, the idea of working from your living room, library, neighbourhood cafe or public park seems somewhat strange. Preconceived notions of work revolve around going to a place markedly different from one's home which has been set aside for activities dedicated for that particular business. Organizations and businesses have built iconic structures which they see as not only as a nexus of work activities, but also an avenue to bolster their brand image and public perception. Many of us have been motivated to work in a particular organization because of the building design.

However, such ideas are being challenged by the new realities of work which like every other new phenomenon is undergoing changes in its definition to suit the current existential needs. Work is now being viewed as what you do and not where you go to. It has really been. But most of us have tied where we go to as work. The morning routine typified by waking up early, rushing out of the door with a handbag in one and coat in another, battling with the morning traffic etc is seen as part of the work. We find it hard to separate the social activities that surround work from the actual work itself.

Managers and organizations insist on having a strict time schedule which implies having their staff arriving and departing at fixed times everyday. Hey! we have even set aside specific days (referred to as work days or business hours) to be clogged up behind a desk or slugging it out in the factory. We believe in the omniscience of a work environment, that space shared with people working towards achieving the single goal of the company.

This inability to dislodge the physical location of work from actual work is the bane of many misconceptions surrounding work. It is possible that one can be the office but not at work. Physical presence does not translate to work essence. As most of us know, it is possible for employees to be lazing around during office hours. In the same vein, it is very possible for people to be productive when they are in informal settings such as coffee shops or cafes.

The crux of the matter is what do u do? Our conceptions of work have shifted from time card and job title to mindset and narrative. This new wave of work pattern is a ripple effect of the present-day knowledge economy where value is placed on knowledge, skills and data. The shift from using physical resources of land, labour and capital as factors of production to abstract ideas to produce goods and services has brought about changes in the way wealth is generated work is executed.

Knowledge resources refer to ideas, innovation or technology which are used to create a product of service. Ideas, just like land and labour have intrinsic economic value. The growth of technology, the spread of creative industries, self-employment and specialized skill-sets are the reflections of a knowledge-based society.

Knowledge resources is the most important resource for the 21st century worker. Emphasis is not placed on credentials or formal trainings, but ideas and specialized skill sets. As such, companies know that the best way to be ahead of the competition and achieve sustainable competitive advantage is by improving on their knowledge base.

Companies such as Google, Netflix and Amazon have been able to been able to propel themselves to the topmost echelon because of their huge base of knowledge resources. They spend huge amount of resources in research and development to bring about innovations that would cater to the ever-changing needs of the consumer. Apart from their shared affinity for knowledge as a fulcrum for organizational growth, these companies also have a flexible workforce. Google in particular represents a classic example of how flexible work patterns can serve as a catalyst for innovation and be used to achieve productivity. The tech giant has been able to tailor its work structure to suit the idiosyncrasies of its workers.

In recent years, organisations have courted the idea of shifting from the conventional nine-to-five work pattern to flexible work arrangements in a bid to sustain competitive advantage, attract the best hands, and remain relevant to the needs of employees and customers. The flexibility of work implies that the boundaries of bureaucracy have been dissolved; and the rigidity that comes with having s structure or chain of command has been eradicated for a free flow of ideas and innovation.

This implies that geographic location does not define work or how it is conducted. Since ideas are intangible assets, and the mode of production has transcended tangible physical and material resources to abstract intangible ones, the way work is executed is most definitely going to be affected. One of the most obvious ways is where people would work from. With the aid of technology, coupled with the unrestrictive nature of labour, it is now possible for people to execute their tasks without stepping into the office or work site. Though some professions require physical presence at a work site such as manufacturing, medical health and construction, the scale of most jobs is tilting towards telecommuting

As such, using place to define notions of work is fast becoming obsolete because working from home is becoming the new reality. Organizations are fast turning to telecommuting to conduct their activities, with some setting up work-from-home initiatives to maintain business continuity and productivity even if their workers are in remote locations. People are leaving their offices for living rooms and coffee shops; swapping work desks for kitchen tables and basements.

Meetings are now being conducted through video conferencing platforms, reports are sent through emails and company platforms while managers are able to monitor work by activity on the company's platform. To ease the conduct of their work, organizations are now providing their staff with tools such as laptops, internet connection, and technology applications.

Working from the office leads to alienation because it forces the individual in question to have two personalities- one at home and one at work. The worker gets separated from work because what (s)he does for a living is disjointed from how (s)he lives. In effect, we are no longer what we do but what people think us to be. Rather than being Tim, Kelly or Dave, we become doctors, engineers and accountants. Conscripting work to an idea of place or location robs us of being ourselves.

In this present age, work can be taken anywhere. While it's not soon that we would see a complete eradication of brick and mortar structures, more businesses would definitely not need a physical office to run. The growing number of freelancers and expansion of gig economy is an exemplification of the future of work. A lot of companies are now engaging freelancers rather than full-time staff because it's a cheaper alternative.

Work is no longer tied to a place or office space. Work is now mobile, transcending geographical boundaries and political contraptions. However, remote working has brought about various effects for health. The flexibility of work schedules has opened up a vista of questions relating to personal health and how people may stay healthy while working from home. The next session deals with the health effects of working from home.

PHYSICAL EFFECTS OF WFH

C hanges in our physical health are the most obvious changes that we notice. Unlike mental and social which are less obvious and deniable, the changes in physical health are changes that occur in our body as a result of what we consume (ingested or inhaled) and degree of our physical activity.

Working from home comes with obvious implications for our physical health. The idea of working in your pyjamas may be the dream of every worker, but being cooped up inside for too long isn't beneficial in the long run. Telecommuting employees should be aware of the need to exercise and keep themselves fit, groomed and eating healthily, especially over extended periods of remote working.

Positive effects of WFH on physical health

· **Exposed to less pollution**: The daily commute to work exposes one to all manners of pollution, most notably sound and air. Inhalation of carbon emissions from vehicles, nauseating alley ways, sharing tight spaces in trains and taxis exposes one to pollution. Because we have reduced our commuting to work, the chances of exposing ourselves to polluted environments is reduced. The serene atmosphere at home (unless of course your kids are at home) helps remote workers to be more productive and reduces distractions.

• **Reduces physical stress**: The physical stress that comes with the daily commute to work is removed allowing us more energy that can be channelled to the execution of task. An average of 3 hours daily is spent on commuting to and from work. Such amount of time implies lost opportunity for productivity. Working from home allows employees to save such precious energy and thus spike their productivity levels.

• **More sleep time**: You don't have to curse and wish you can get a few extra minutes of snooze time when you work from home. Working from home in many ways reduces the need for such a rigid sleep and wake up time, partly because you no longer have a commute to contend with. Since you are in control of your work time, you are bound to get more sleep time.

Negative Effects on Physical Health

Working from home also comes with adverse consequences for our physical health. These are treated below.

Lack of exercise: Physical inactivity is the most obvious effect of working from home. Lack of exercise is termed to be as dangerous as smoking. Spending long hours behind a laptop means less physical activity for us. This leads to health complications such as obesity, diabetes and high blood pressure. A sedentary life style incurs the risk of many cancers.

Weight gain: Due to the sedentary lifestyle that comes with working from home, there is a very high probability that we would out on weight because of limited physical activity. There is also the temptation of compulsive snacking and overeating since the kitchen is just a few steps away. While it is also tough to motivate yourself to leave the comfort of your house to exercise, for those who exercise, working from home can disrupt work-out schedules.

Not enough sleep: When we work from home, the boundaries between work and private life tend to be blurred. Sharing our private space with work means we don't have a commute to deal with and no rigid sleep routine to adhere to. This also means it may be more difficult to switch off from work because there would be no demarcation between work time. There is always the tendency to want to complete one more task or answer to one more email. Adding one more thing and postponing the closing time adds to the levels of stress and anxiety. It can also be hard to wind down and fall asleep at night time, when you've been at home all day. Fresh air, exercise, and social interaction all play a part in helping us to feel 'tired enough' to sleep.

MENTAL EFFECTS
OF WFH

Mental effects of working from home are more pronounced but less obvious. The paradigm shift that comes with changes in the traditional mode of work has several effects on the mental health of the telecommuter. First, we examine the benefits.

Mental benefits of WFH

No more toxic environment

One of the major health benefits of working from home is not having to deal with toxic work environment. Working alone means being away from chaotic co-workers, back-stabbing colleagues and annoying supervisors. You don't have to deal with the office gossip and endless chatter. You don't have to be a player in the office politics going on. It means that you are in charge of your health.

Boosts independence and self-confidence

Working alone means that there is no safety support net for you to fall back on when you get confused on how to execute certain task to solve certain work-related issues. As such it provides a learning curve upon which we can trust our decisions more and enhance our self-confidence. The joy that comes with executing tasks unaided implies that we are growing in competence and efficiency. It makes us believe in our capability in getting the job done.

Maturity and discipline

If we are able to stick to a routine without an overbearing supervisor watching over us, it bespeaks of maturity and self-discipline. It shows that we can work with little supervision and as such makes our superiors trust us the more. What's more, it puts us on the path of self-discovery. As we work away, isolated from colleagues and superiors we tend to communicate with ourselves on a deeper level. We get to know how to balance our talents and flaws to make us more productive. We know when we are most productive and when we would churn out trash work. We know what approach or strategy best works for us rather than following rules and procedures that may be antithetical to our personality and talents. In summary, we get to know ourselves better which makes us more matured and disciplined in our actions.

Reduced work-related stress

Working from home also reduces stress which comes as a result of working from a designated office. Commuting to work, working under pressure to meet deadlines and targets, or having co-workers sharing your office space are some factors that trigger stress at work. Working from home insulates one from all these, forming a protective cocoon around one's mentation.

Time Management

As a remote worker, you can schedule your day and time as you see fit. Remote work allows you to choose your work flow because you structure your activities according to the demands of the day. This autonomy improves your mental wellbeing because it allows you peace of mind to handle your needs as they come up, structuring your day and work to maximize your efficiency. An offshoot of this is the freedom and autonomy that comes with telecommuting which adds immeasurable value to your mental health. Being in control of one's time and life put you in a high pedestal of mental wellbeing.

Job Satisfaction

Those who work from home have reported higher levels of job Satisfaction than those who do not. This is according to a study carried out by the MIT Sloane School of Management. Due to reduced levels of psychological stress and burnouts; and being able to spend more time with family, control over work schedule, remote workers are reporting higher levels of job satisfaction.

Negative mental effects of WFH

Here are the most commonly reported issues that remote workers and digital nomads face:

Loneliness and isolation

Most remote workers face loneliness and isolation because the social aspect of work has been yanked off. You could spend days not talking to anyone when you don't have to go anywhere to work. This is not healthy for our mental health as communication with others has been shown to reinforce our sense of wellbeing and our belonging in the community. Research has shown that loneliness and isolation is twice as harmful to physical and mental health as obesity.

Loneliness is also associated with higher rates of depression, anxiety, and somatic symptoms like random pain. Although you bypass distracting co-workers, you do miss the social aspect of chatting and venting about work and life when you're remote. This camaraderie doesn't translate the same way over.

Isolation also comes from the feeling of been left out of the things that are happening in the office. A study of 1153 remote workers conducted by the *Harvard Business Review* found that the 52% of them were more likely to feel left out and mistreated by the colleagues who went to the office. This led to mistrust and eventually affected their productivity at work. If there is no one to form a basis of comparism or talk to when feeling stressed or challenged at work, it could rebound and affect our efficiency.

Depression

Working from home can also trigger bouts of depression. This comes from feelings of being stuck and not advancing in one's life. While in offices and formal organizations, it is easier to measure or progress or success by promotions, pay rises, an official car with a driver, or increased responsibilities. Without career milestones like a new nameplate on your desk or a fancy corner office, it is easy to feel as if you're not achieving as much as your peers.

Mental stagnation

We know that iron sharpeneth iron. The easiest way to imbibe a character or trait is by placing yourself in an environment that fosters such trait. Working in an office with colleagues means that one is exposed to the latest trends, news, strategies and tactics. This implies that by communicating with co-workers, our mental development increase because of the plethora of information available to us. Such perks may be missing when one works from home.

Unless you are an information junkie, one may be operating with obsolete information because the information pipeline has been turned off. We may suffer from mental stagnation without appropriate communication with others. Worse still, it would take us longer times to decipher current trends or strategies thereby making us lose valuables time and reducing out productivity level.

Stress, anxiety and pressure

Though working from home can lower anxiety levels, it can also exacerbate it. This is most especially true when we do not have any control measures in place. According to a 2017 study of remote working in 15 countries conducted by the United Nations, 41 percent of "highly mobile" employees considered themselves highly stressed in comparism to only 25 percent of those that worked in offices.

Work from home anxiety comes from over working and not knowing when to switch off, taking up on multiple freelance jobs at once, procrastinating from completing. Stress may also be induced by an overreliance on mobile devices and technology and technological tools to execute tasks. Higher stress levels have been linked to reliance on smartphones and laptops which invariably leads to greater social isolation and even insomnia.

Misconception about WFH

One of the mental clogs that telecommuters face is the inability of other people to conceptualize working from home as a "real job". Most people don't place value on remote working as much as an in-office job. It is not out of place for partners or parents to ask "when will you finally get a REAL job again?" The fact that you may be working more hours at home than an in-office job does little to change their misconception. As such, you may find your partner or parent trying to assign chores to you since you are "less busy".

SOCIAL EFFECTS OF WFH

Humans are social animals and we depend on our social network to define our essence as human beings. Since we tend to spend most of our time at work, our offices have also become a major part of that complex web that makes up our social life. Most workers build relationships with colleagues that go beyond the walls of the company. We get to meet new people in the form of colleagues and customers; our kids go to the same school as our colleagues' kids, our wives belong to the same community groups etc. It's no wonder that when faced with working from home, our social life is impacted. This comes with both positive and negative effects.

Social benefits of WFH

Prioritize our relationships with others

Despite living the life of a hermit, WFH tends to come with social benefits. One of such is that it allows us to know what relationships to people to prioritize in our lives. When left with ourselves, and away from the noise and distraction of everyday life, we tend to reflect and ponder on the crucial things of life. The relationships or people that mean much to us tend to become the focus of our thoughts. We separate our friends from colleagues. Also, we know those whom we are dear to and live our company. Colleagues who check up on you regularly and who always maintain communication are those we should be closer to, because out of sight doesn't mean out of mind for them.

Allows us time to build social bonds

WFH frees up a huge chunk of our time which would have erstwhile been used to develop social bonds in other areas. Busy work schedules has prevented a lot of people from developing healthy social relationships with their children, spouse or parents. Remote working defuses any excuse that keeps us way from. Devoting time to our families and lived ones making us to forge deeper social connection with close ones. As such, the weight of our social scale which tilted heavily towards work would balance out as we spend more time with family and loved ones.

Make new friends

Since our work is now mobile and not conscripted to a single building or place, this gives remote workers the opportunity to explore the world around them, and make new friends in the process. A lot of people's conventional jobs affects their social life, restricting it to a circle of colleagues or people from the same industry. As such, we find out that during our leisure time, discussions still tend to hover around work. Meeting new people form diverse backgrounds enables us get a wider perspective towards life and a more rounded outlook. We also get to visit places we haven't seen or always wanted to, making us live a rich and diverse life.

Negative Social Effects of WFH

Social Isolation

The most obvious social effect of working from home is the disconnection from your social network. The office is a hub of social interaction. A good amount of work occurs when people gather together to chit chat and brain storm. That's how people know the latest trends or share ideas on how to approach a problem or resolve an issue. Staying home means less communication and less space for social networking. As such, we are disconnected from the wider social circle. Though we can catch up with video, cheating and phone calls, nothing beats the depth of interaction that comes from face to face communication.

Less comradery

WFH breaks up the social cohesion that we would have with other colleagues which comes as a result of shared everyday experiences. WFH means no more commuting, no more small talk, and hardly any in-person interaction at all, as such no comradery. Colleagues who were bounded by a shared common experience that an office provides would now see themselves as separate beings just working to complete a task. It also has implications for the culture of an organization as it would be more difficult for companies to be able to instil and uphold values on workers who are not physically present.

Makes communication mechanical

Because we are living anti-social lifestyles necessitated by working from home, we tend to lose our social skills over time. Our social skills give way to mechanical skills in which we communicate without emotions. This may not be necessarily due to the remote worker, but the communication tools which are available this present time. Communication through email and texts takes off the emotional factor. Even visual tools such as video chat, tend to make us guarded and keep our emotions in check rather than being free and vent our feelings. This kills the fabric of truthful communication which entails passing the exact message we want across. Sometimes the message we want to pass cannot be transmitted through words but emotions and body language. This aspect tends to be numbed while using techno-logical tools.

We may hurt close ones

Working from home means closed ones may be up in our faces all the time. As you prepare to settle down in your little workspace corner, that may be the time your 4-year old daughter would want to play hide and week or your spouse may want to engage in an 'important' discussion. You need to get work done so you push them away or snub them. Of course, they would feel bad and hurt and then to misinterpret your actions. All these steam from the fact that people still battle with their perception of work. When one works from home, it is not viewed as work. As such, private matters tend to creep in during 'office' hours which if not handled with fact would bring about conflict.

HEALTHY WAYS
OF WFH

While WFH seems to be the new reality following the current turndown in global economy due to the corona virus pandemic, what are the ways in which people can work from home without compromising their physical, mental or social health. Below are some of the ways one can work from home without mortgaging any aspect pf their health.

Physical Healthy ways of WFH

WFH is a portal to a sedentary lifestyle which could have culminative adverse effects for your wellbeing. Below are some ways to ensure that your physical health does not suffer while you work from home.

Get an ergonomic (Kinesis) keyboard

Kinesis keyboards and accessories help address ulnar deviation and forearm pronation, two repetitive issues that comes with using traditional keyboards. Ulnar deviation, also known as ulnar drift, refers to a medical condition that causes the joints in the wrist and hand to bend outwards towards the little finger which causes the carpal tunnel in the wrist to constrict. Ulnar deviation causes swelling and pain in the wrist and finger joints thereby reducing the grip strength of the hand and limiting the finger's range of motion. Forearm pronation on the other hand refers to the downward orientation of the forearm. When your forearm faces down, it is said to be pronated.

Because the conventional keyboard is flat and straight while your arms are not, typing on it requires the user to face his palms downward which pronates the forearm and wrists. You also need to twist your wrists outwards so that your hands are roughly parallel If such postures are sustained, this increases pressure on the forearm muscles and surrounding tissues leading to reduction in the circulation of blood which invariably causes fatigue and injury.

An ergonomic keyboard addresses this postural hazard. These revolutionized keyboard designs reduce the pain associated with forearm pronation and lowers the risk of ulnar deviation. By altering the placement of the keys on the board, one does not have to swivel your wrists to type. keyboards such as *Microsoft Comfort* and *Sculpt* keyboards maintain the conventional keyboard style but with added ergonomic features that make typing fun. More revolutionary ergonomic keyboard designs such as *Kinesis Freestyle 2* and *Kinesis maxim* split the traditional keyboard into two, separating the keys into two boards which can be adjusted to any angle. This means that keys on the left-hand side of the board can be placed at a different angle from the keys on the right-hand side. This latter type of keyboards allows the user to split the keyboard to the desired width that works perfectly for his arms. They also help to manage space on the desk.

Get a proper office chair and desk

Let's face it. Our homes do not have proper office chairs that allow us to work for long period of time. Most of us are forced to improvise by using the kitchen counter, coffee table or even bathroom as our office space. Working for extended periods of time in our improvised office spaces and hunched in compromising positions is not great for your body and overall health. This implies that we have to be cognisant of our posture while working.

A good way of alleviating the stress and pain that comes from improper postures is by getting a good chair. Going for chairs with adjustable features, such as seat height, back rest, arm rests and lumbar support, is help with comfort and ergonomics. lumbar support pillows also bring extra comfort to sitting positions, though you can improvise with just any pillow - even a towel would suffice. Just roll it and place between the chair and your neck or back, or on the seat to give you extra height. If you can, get a chair on wheels as this allows you to maintain an appropriate distance away from your computer so that you can stretch your arms and legs.

Take regular screen breaks

Not just to stretch your arms and legs, but to protect your eyes too. Because we are working from home, we tend to be deeply immersed in our work that we don't realize how fast time goes. Sustaining long hours behind the laptop is not a good idea. It is important that we take regular breaks to refresh our minds and allow our muscles relax. You can set a timer to go off every hour to take a break for fifteen minutes. Walking frees up the creative juices and keeps it flowing. You also get to stretch your cramped-up muscles. So, it's advisable to walk around, or do some quick stretches. If you are the type that gets to immersed in work, apps like *TimeOut* or *Smart Break* help you to manage your break time efficiently.

Monitor your eating habits

One of the perks of working from home is that you get to do

whatever you want. Literally. Food is never far away from you, and it could be your worst enemy. You can over-indulge or starve yourself of food altogether. These two extremes are not healthy and could affect productivity at work. As such, there is need to take cognisance of where, what, and how you eat when working from home. Firstly, eat away from your work desk. Turning your home office into a mini cafeteria is not the best idea. It is also not advisable to work from the kitchen as this could increase your craving for food and make one over-indulge. Eat your meals in your regular place away from your work desk. Minimize your intake of coffee. Working from home has a tendency to make us binge drink on coffee to boost morale and stay alert for the work. Water is a healthy substitute to drenching yourself in caffeine. More about eating while working from home is treated ion the later section of this book.

Set a routine for yourself

In the conventional office setting, it's easier to have a routine because there is a designated time for resuming and closing work. You get to be paid overtime if you even spend more hours working. At home, the scenario is quite different as the time between resumption and closing is blurred if not completely extinguished. Setting a routine does not only have mental benefits, but also physical ones too. Establishing a routine implies that you have time designated to engage yourself in various tasks including resting your body. This helps to keep your acitvites in check and not allow you become totally immersed in your work to the detriment of your physical health. Routine makes sure that you designate appropriate time for sleep.

Exercise regularly

Ensure that you exercise regularly to burn those extra calories you may have picked up because of long hours of inactivity. Walking, running, stretching, push-ups—whatever works for you

– helps to reduce stress. It also makes blood circulate around your body and frees up those muscles that may have cramped up during those long hours behind the computer. You can't underestimate the importance of exercise if you work remotely.

Mental Healthy ways of WFH

Your mental health is what gets affected the most following the transition to working from home. At first, you may be happy to be away from nosey colleague and annoying office politics. However, after a while you begin to miss human interaction, which of course tends to affect you mentally. Here are strategies for working from home in ways that are beneficial to your mental health.

Have a to-do-list

Scheduling is an intricate part of working from home. It is so easy to get lost in the vicissitudes of remote working since you don't have a boss or supervisor breathing down your neck. Since you feel you have the whole day to yourself, there is the tendency to procrastinate, or ease up on the gas pedal once you have completed a task. Having a list of tasks to complete enables you to maintain focus, enhances productivity and allows you to deal with stress in appropriate ways. Make a list every morning or at the 'close' of work to prepare you for the tasks ahead. Setting goals and time limits for each task is a simple but effective and fulfilling technique. Apps such as *Toggle*, *Todoist* and *TickTick* help you to stay organised and focused.

Get a dedicated workspace

Getting a dedicated space within the home for work tends to put you mentally 'in the zone' for work. Such space should not include the bedroom or kitchen and definitely not in front of the television. Try to work from the same spot every day. Even if you are holed up in a one-room shack, you can create a favourite corner to work from. The key is having a workspace that enables you to function efficiently. You can even decorate by adding flowers, pictures and music. Just make sure your workspace is a place where you can focus and churn out your best work. A place you enjoy going to everyday.

Set Boundaries

It is absolutely necessary to establish boundaries and set ground rules with family members and friends when working from home as this reduces distraction. It is easy to be distracted by house chores or any domestic issue that my crop up. Family members tend to think that working from home means you are always available. Lay down rules for who can enter your workspace and when. Set ground rules with other people in your home or who share your space for when you work. If you have children around let them know that your workspace is off limits for certain periods of the day. You need space to work and produce, constant distractions from co habitants would truncate the wave of productivity. Communicate your schedule to everyone.

Structure your day like you would in the office.

It's easy to lose focus when you are not in an office setting. The meetings, chatter with colleagues, constant follow-up from superiors who watch you like a hawk, and periodic appraisals tend to keep one in check and make them put more effort in their jobs. All these are absent in remote working. As complacency and laxity tend to set in. We may clock in less our than we do at the office. This is a pitfall that robs many remote workers of productivity. It is advisable to structure your day like you would in your office. Resume and close by the usual time. Proceed to go on break the same time as you would have done while in office. If an issue which interrupts your work crops up, there are flexible ways of handling this whole still putting in the same amount of time in your office work. If you work 8 or 12 hours a day, you can also clock in that same amount of time. The only difference is that you may not do it at a single stretch as you would do in the office. You can work for 3 hours, then proceed on a break, then come back to work. If you leave the home to handle an emergency or errand, make a metal note of how much time you have put in the work, then balance up those hours when you return. That way you still out in the same number of hours as those in the office.

Break the pressure circuit

A 2017 report published by *European Foundation for the Improvement of Living and Working Conditions* observed that a higher percentage of remote employees reported higher levels of stress compared to their counterparts who worked in the office. Remote working comes with the added pressure of wanting to prove to your superiors that you being productive. This makes you to go out of our ways to please our supervisors. One way of doing this is trying to complete as many tasks as possible within the shortest possible time, thereby putting yourself under undue pressure. Putting oneself under such pressure constantly would definitely boomerang on your mental health. This is why breaks are important for remote workers. If you feel the pressure from work piling up, you can shut down and go for a walk to clear your brain and catch some fresh air. You can also play music to sooth your nerves and calm your emotions. You could also call a friend or video chat a loved one to distract your mind from the pressure of work.

Avoid setting high expectations

Just because we are our own boss doesn't mean that we should immediately aim for the stars or shoot for the moon. Such notions only personify pressure and make us binge on disappointments. We should be humble with little beginnings and see the completion of every task as a journey and not a destination. Let us learn how to celebrate small victories but without losing sight of the bigger goals. It is okay to fail, what matters is our reaction to failure. One good thing of not having high expectations is that we take failure in good faith. However, we mut be cautious of degenerating into indolence so that we do not use our low expectations as an excuse.

Check-up on co-workers

Even though remote working takes you away from the office politics, at a time you begin to miss the office chatter and gossip. Its normal to check up on co-workers and see how they are catching up. Nurturing relationships is crucial for your metal health, let alone when working remotely. It helps to relive pressure because it is refreshing to be able to share your pain with someone who understands your situation. Who else than your co-worker? Communication with colleagues helps you feel less isolated and fuels productivity.

Know when to shut down

To preserve your mental health, it is absolutely necessary to know when to shut down and leave work behind. This is not only restricted to shutting down your laptop and leaving your work desk, but also refraining from all sorts of work-related communication during non-working hours. This enables your brain to refresh, your body to relax and your mind to mediate on other things that make you a human being, not just work. Besides taking time off work makes you come back refreshed and with new ideas.

Get a life

Because you work from home, there is the tendency to slip into a triangular way of life. Eat, sleep and work. This pattern of life cocoons us from the rest of the world, turning us into hermits and reducing the humanity in us. Work has to be balanced with play and fun. Make time for other aspects of your life. Go visiting extended family members, make out time for social activities. Take the weekends off to catch up on movies and games. Engage in community service. You could travel and be way from your laptop for some period of time. The key is to start living!!!! Work is only one part of having a well-rounded life. The other parts should not suffer because you have invited your work to share your private space. It is necessary to set boundaries and rules so as to avoid distractions when working from home, but it is equally important, if not more, to know when to draw the line between work and other areas of your life. Variety they say is the spice of life. Talk to other people who don't do the same work as you.

SOCIAL HEALTHY WAYS OF WFH

Working from home also affects our social life. This is probably the first part of our health that gets affected before it transcends to the mental part. Interaction with other people is an intricate part of our humanity. Working from home denies us of this chance to express our humanity by keeping us away from others. However, there are steps we can take to ensure that we maintain our social health while remote working. These steps have already been outlined in the previous section that dealt with mental health. For example, communicating with colleagues ensures that we our social relationships do not suffer because we are away from our colleagues. We can dedicate weekends to go for movies, visit art exhibitions or organize a family dinner. As human beings we need an appropriate social network that one can fall back on when the pressure of society pushes us. Whatever start we apply to improve our mental health while working from home invariably affects our social life. The aim is building a work culture that would not be detrimental to any aspect of our health.

HOW TO WORK EFFECTIVELY FROM HOME

W orking effectively from home means setting yourself up to be productive. This entails having the right tools and environment that would enhance your productivity. You have to also have ways of dealing with kids, kids, pets, and other potential disruptions. Below are steps to work from home in an efficient manner.

Maintain a consistent work schedule

Consistency is the bedrock of efficiency. Once we have set up a routine and a habit, it is easy to get into the flow even though we do not feel like it. It is easy to be seduced by the notion of flexibility, but if we are inconsistent with our work schedules, it is a great disservice to our productivity. Maintaining a consistent work schedule makes you accountable to yourself. You are more likely to get much done if you are consistent with your work schedule.

Choose your most productive hour

Some are slow starters; others jump right off the block. We

all have our work preferences and the time of the day when we are most productive. Some people prefer to be the early morning birds, others wait till midday before they come out of their sleepy hibernation, while others are nocturnal beings like owls. Provided your boss does not give you a time schedule or the demands of your job does not require you to be behind your computer at a specific time of the day, it is best to work when you are at your productive zenith. Trying to work when you are least productive is like forcing a horse to drink from the stream. If your mind is misaligned from the task at hand, this creates room for mistakes and affects your efficiency. Knowing your most productive time of the day makes you get much done in less time.

Get the right tools

A bad workman complains of his tools. But if you don't have the right tools you would be a bad workman. Getting the right tools to set up your home office is as important as your mental state. The right tools can make or mar your efficiency and ability to deliver on the job. High speed Internet connection, gadgets, headsets, computers, hard drives, wireless mouse and even your work desk affect how you are able to work and at what rate. Some companies bear this burden by providing their remote workers with equipment that would ease their work. As a remote worker, there are a plethora of tools that can enable you work efficiently. *Zoom* and *Skype* for video conferencing; *Toggle* for time management, *LastPass* for security are just some examples that can make your work easy.

Practice self-control

This has been dealt with in previous sessions of this book. However, there is need to emphasize minimizing distractions at your home workplace because It's easy to get distracted especially when left to your own devices. Distractions make come from kids, neighbours or pets, but it can also be internal. We have to have a good measure of self-control if we are to work efficiently from home. This implies staying away from your phone, social media the television or internet. It also implies not taking undeserved breaks or postponing work. Mindless scrolling of phones for juicy gossip on social media is a serious time waster. Focus on the task at hand and tell yourself you are not finished until you are done. You can put your phone on airplane mode, hide the TV remote and work only from a designated office space in your home. Better still, you can download productivity apps such as *Todoist, Trello* or *Forest*, if you're finding it hard to focus from home, productivity apps.

Track Your Progress

Keeping close tabs on your progress is another strategy that can help you work efficiently, having a to-do list is not a guarantee for productivity and efficiency. There is need to revisit and reflect on previous way and task ourselves on ways that we can accomplish them better. Do not set high expectations, but it would do you a lot of good to keep questioning yourself on how you can execute your tasks efficiently. This reduces time spent procrastinating and enables you to focus on your job.

Do not break the work flow

This is analogous to choosing the time of the day when you are most productive. When you find yourself in the zone and your creative juices are flowing, please do not break the flow to have a snack, rest or make a phone call. Doing so would only hurt your progress. Being in the zone means that your mind and soul are aligned with the task at hand. It is a difficult place to get to, and more difficult to sustain. However, whenever we do get there, the pace of our work quickens, likewise the quality which improves drastically. As such, whenever, we find ourselves we are in that zone, we should delay taking the exit route as much as possible so that we can get much done.

Avoid working on an empty stomach

Try and eat a hearty meal before starting off for the day. Make sure to never skip lunch. An empty stomach means an empty brain, which is bad for productivity. give yourself a much-needed break to fuel and refuel your batteries before and during work. But it is important that you have your meals away from your work area, so that as you are eating, your brain and mind can also refuel with the much needed rest. This brings us to the next session.

EATING HEALTHY WHEN YOU'RE WORKING FROM HOME

B alancing work and life is a herculean task for most people when working from the office, let alone when they share the same space. One of the things that gets affected when we work from home is our eating habit. It is easy to buy into the illusion that working from home means you would be eating healthy. Most starters to remote working believe that the working away from the office means less eat-outs, junk food, sugar and calories. The idea of working from home paints the picture that we would be have more of home-cooked meals with fresh ingredients.

However, there are several factors that could make us eat in proportions that are unhealthy for our body. When unhealthy eating is mentioned, the preconceived notion is that we may be taking in too much fat or calorie which leads to weight gain. Nonetheless, unhealthy eating comes in three-fold. Unhealthy eating entails overeating, undereating, and malnutrition.

A remote worker is susceptible to one or more of these forms of unhealthy eating. one of the factors that exacerbates unhealthy eating habits is flexibility of work pattern. The way we work influences our eating habits. Flexibility of work patterns brings about flexibility in when, where and how we eat. The absence of routine that comes with working from home if not properly checked would lead to non-routinized eating patterns. Traditional work pattern tends to restrict our eating habits because we have to be at our desks or duty posts. We tend to adhere to a strict timeline for meals when we are at the office. Most of us have breakfast, have a specific time for lunch, and dinner when we get home. Working from home implies you can just waltz into the kitchen to have whatever you want.

When working from home, because we do not have 'opening' and 'closing' hours, we tend to not have a fixed time to have our meals. The omnipresence of your computer which constantly states us in the face makes some of us jump right into the work before we think of having anything. We skip breakfast for work.

The pressure of work is another factor that promotes unhealthy eating habits while working from home. In a bid to meet deadlines and complete task, there is the tendency to skip meals because of the perception that food is only an arm's length away. We go long hours before having anything to eat, skipping regular meals altogether resorting to quick fixes which are either unhealthy or undernourished, when the pang of hunger reminds them to eat because they are scared that taking time off to eat may break the momentum of the work. As such, our eating patterns become erratic and ill-timed for the body. when we eventually get to it, we tend to overeat to make up for the meals that we have skipped.

For others, food becomes a useful side-kick anytime they want to take their mind off work or encounter a challenge which requires them to think. They develop cravings anytime the mind gets distracted from work. As such, they tend to over-indulge themselves in their cravings. Yet some like to have a little snack to keep the mouth bust while working. To this set of workers, food is a useful companion for work.

Close proximity to the kitchen also doesn't help. Some home offices are set up in the kitchen table with the refrigerator constantly stating you in the face and nudging you. This is an entirely bad idea because it is one of the easiest ways to indulge in binge eating while working from home.

The crux of the matter is that without a schedule, and the will to adhere to it, there is a probability of eating mindlessly throughout the day, or waiting too long to eat is very high. As such, there are strategies which can help one eat healthy while working from home.

WFH Strategies for eating healthy

Develop a eating schedule

Having a schedule for your meals should be factored in whenever plans are being made for work. If you are one of those who are deeply engrossed in their work that you forget about eating then having a meal schedule is not a bad idea. This way, you don't skip having those nutritive meals that are needed by your body. Just as you would have a to-do-list if tasks to complete, having an eating schedule should be a part of our plans. This enables us to keep in track and not deviate whenever we get a craving. You should have a definite time for main meals, lunch breaks, snack times etc. After a while, your stomach would get used to these times and adjust accordingly. One way to do this is setting alarms in our computers and phones to remind you when it's time to eat. Taking a break take every 2 ½ to 3 hours to eat/snack is okay.

Ensure your food nutrient is balanced

This includes having fruits, vegetables, protein, carbohydrates, iron and vitamins. Your meal does not have to contain all these nutrients. But one should have a healthy dose of each of them daily. Fruits, salads, oatmeals or homemade granola bars are good starters for having a balanced diet.

Always have Breakfast

For most remote workers, the routine may involve waking up and getting straight to work instead of performing your usual morning rituals. Part of the morning ritual includes eating breakfast. Always ensure that you have breakfast before starting off work because this is the most important meal of the day. Starting the day with a good meal energizes you to face the rest of the day. you are also less likely to graze until it's time for a break. Even if you don't feel like eating, you can always have a small breakfast before lunchtime.

Snack in a healthy way

Snacks give us the boost of energy we need to get through the day. Working from home makes it hard to avoid snacking. The most appropriate time to have a snack is between lunch and dinner as it gives you that final burst to finish your work and cook dinner. However, your snacks should be healthy. Instead of sweet and salty foods, healthy alternatives such as smoothies or fruits would so your body a whole lot of good. Having a bowl of fruit or a bag of carrots or nuts on your desk is not a bad idea if you intend to graze during the day. Since snacks are a quick fix, the likelihood of grabbing what's in front of you instead of walking down to the kitchen is high.

Plan Your Lunch

Planning your lunch is equally important too. It reduces the likelihood of having an unhealthy lunch or snack. It also reduces the amount of time you would have spent on planning and eating lunch during work hours.

More Water, less caffeine

One of the consequences of remote working is over indulgence in our work. Since we do not have official work hours, we tend to spend more time at work. One of the ways we use to boost ourselves while going for this long stretch of time is coffee. Nonetheless, drinking too much coffee can have side effects for our health. Rather than binge drinking coffee we can always take water. A large glass of water at your desk is all it takes. Water helps to keep us dehydrated, aids digestion and flushes our system. If you feel you can't do without your favourite cup of coffee, then try limiting your daily intake. Tea is also a good substitute for coffee. Listen to your body and drink whenever you feel thirsty.

Out with the Junk Food

If you know you want to snack in a healthy way, then it's best that you get rid of the junk food in your house. Clear out your kitchen of processed food and unhealthy snacks. Stock up your fridge with fruits, vegetables, yogurt, chicken, and fish. If you have junk food in your kitchen, you can keep them. Out of sight by hiding them in cabinets to avoid temptation. alternatively, you could also put healthy snack options in front of you so that you would be less tempted to have an unhealthy snack.

Eat away from your work desk

Not many people think that eating demands some amount of concentration. That is why we do not eat mindfully. Because of the informal nature of working from home, we tend to eat and work simultaneously. This robs us of the opportunity to enjoy the food and savour it's richness. Besides eating at your work desk doesn't give you the full satisfaction of having a meal. This is why you don't work in the kitchen and don't eat at your work place. The two should be mutually exclusive.

Are you hungry or is it a craving?

It is not unusual to have food cravings. However, if we are unable to control ourselves and manage our cravings, it could lead to overeating thereby making us gain weight in unhealthy ways. So how does one differentiate hunger from craving? You begin to feel the pang of hunger if you haven't eaten for a few hours. The sensation tends to increase with time causing your stomach to growl. You also experience a headache and fatigue when you are hungry, plus you would be willing to eat anything.

On the other hand, a craving may be described as a flash in the pan. It appears intermittently, even after you have just eaten. Cravings are usually satisfied with snacks or small meals. Cravings can be quenched by either having a small meal or distracting your mind. Hunger can only be quenched by food. When you have a craving you can go for a walk, have a glass of water or even play a game. Cravings may also result from stress. If we have a challenge at work or feel pressured, we may have cravings to eat as a way of dealing with the stress. learning to identify the triggers which cause us to crave for food is important as it makes us more aware of the situation and indulge less in food. In the worst-case scenario, when we have cravings we can indulge in healthier options such as eating fruits.

WORK FROM HOME: FUTURE APPROACHES

There is no doubt that remote working represents the future of the work place. For many organizations, this means embracing the new notions of work and seeking how to maintain efficiency and productivity without compromising on quality. For the worker, it means applying a strict routine to ensure productivity is not sacrificed on the altar of comfort of home distraction. Whatever may be the case, the reality is that remote working is the future of the workplace. It is a direct consequence of the knowledge economy we now operate whereby ideas are traded as commodities and globalization has blurred physical and political boundaries. Remote working also blurs the idea of time for organizations that have identified this potential. With technology it is possible to get different people across time zones to work in projects. So rather than restricting work to specific time of the day, workers can organise themselves depending on the time zone to get the work going.

There would also be a definite shift in the skill market. Though traditional occupations such as carpentry, masonry, medicine and mechanic would still exist, there would be a demand for new skills. We are already seeing this in the demand surge for skills such as content writing, web designing, graphic design, animation and programming. This implies that there would be a radical shift for soft skills.

The corona virus pandemic has also made remote working more acceptable as most organizations now favour working from home because of its health and cost benefits. This calls for new responsibilities from supervisors and HR managers. Gone are the days when managers believe that suspicion of subordinates and constant monitoring was a prerequisite for a effective management. Supervisors would have to learn to trust their subordinates if they expect them to deliver on their job. HR managers would also have to resort to newer means of interviewing and verifying workers other than the conventional ways. A look at the candidate's social media page seems the way to go. Though experience and skills would matter, other values such as empathy, honesty, initiative and creativity would matter the most in this new era. The fog is yet to clear, as such there would be many learning points as we adjust to this work patter. The key is being open minded and receptive to whatever change comes.

ABOUT THE AUTHOR

Derrick Chandler

Derrick Chandler is the pen name of Chika Nwakanma, a seasoned medical anthropologist that has written on a number of topics ranging from health to politics

BOOKS BY THIS AUTHOR

Taking The Dope Out Of Dopamine

This book looks at the chemical behind our cravings and addictions and suggests healthy ways of having a deox

Tackling Gaming Disorder: How Parents Can Help Their Kids Deal With Video Game Addiction

This books looks at the reasons kids are addicted to video games and how parents can help their kids curb this menace